Growing
in the
Glory

I0176712

by

Carol Hylton

Growing in the Glory
Copyright © 2014 by Carol Hylton

Unless otherwise noted, all Scripture references are from *The Holy Bible, New King James Edition*, copyright © 1979, 1980, 1982, by Thomas Nelson, Inc., Nashville, Tennessee. References marked "KJV" are from *The Holy Bible, Authorized King James Version*. References marked "NASB" are from the *New American Standard Bible*, copyright © 1960, 1962, 1963, 1968, 1971, 1972, 1973, 1975, 1977 by the Lockman Foundation, La Habra, California.

Cover Image: Disaster in the Haiti Earthquake
by Woodthon Felix

Published by:

McDougal & Associates
18896 Greenwell Springs Road
Greenwell Springs, Louisiana 70739
www.ThePublishedWord.com

McDougal & Associates is an organization dedicated to the spreading the Gospel of the Lord Jesus Christ to as many people as possible in the shortest time possible.

ISBN 978-1-940461-14-4

Printed on demand in the U.S., the UK, and Australia
For worldwide distribution

Growing
in the
Glory

McDougal & Associates
Servants of Christ and Stewards of the
Mysteries of God

At Tabbare, Haiti, during my 2010 mission trip

Then the Lord answered me and said:

"Write the vision
And make it plain on tablets,
That he may run who reads it.
For the vision is yet for an appointed time!"

Habakkuk 2:2-3

ACKNOWLEDGMENTS

I would like to thank my editor and all my mentors who have inspired me over time to pursue my dreams, with special thanks to Fay Montgomery, who encouraged me to write this book. I especially want to thank my mom and my grandmother, who gave me the liberty to grow in the glory!

CONTENTS

FOREWORD BY BETHLEHEM HAILE

Understanding the unique and powerful plan of God for our lives gives us a sense of dignity, purpose, courage, and compassion that He alone can construct. When I was introduced to the book, *Growing in the Glory*, I couldn't stop reading. There is an anointing upon every chapter of its message. I believe many will be delivered and be anointed to worship as they read this book.

Every believer needs to know that worshiping in the midst of our trials will bring deliverance in every area of our lives. Pastor Carol, thank you so much for waking me up at 4:00 A.M. each morning to join the daily prayer, for I know it will help me to keep *Growing in the Glory.*

Bethlehem Haile
Centennial, Colorado

FOREWORD BY FAY MONTGOMERY

I have known Carol Hylton since the early 1990s. The glory of God was on her life then, and through the years it has only increased and filled her to overflowing. When a person spends time in His presence, His glory is evident in them.

I believe that what Carol is writing here is coming from a heart filled with that glory and am convinced that all those who read it will receive an impartation of this same glory, as they allow the Holy Spirit to work in their life as it has in Carol's.

Just as Peter walked by people in the first century and his shadow healed the sick it touched, I believe that the words of this book will bring you deeper into God's presence today.

Rev. Fay Montgomery

INTRODUCTION

As Christians, we are all called to be salt and light to the world around us, witnesses for Christ. For many years now I have been blessed to be able to do that, not only here at home (New York), but also in parts of this country and many other nations of the world.

As I have traveled, I have always discovered opportunities in which I could make a difference, opportunities to change the lives of the men and women I encountered. And that's what it's all about. In this way, we become the Lord's ambassadors, His representatives, speaking His Word and being His hands extended to bless and heal.

God has promised great things for the days ahead. He said:

"The glory of this latter temple [house, KJV] shall be greater than the former," says the L<small>ORD</small> of hosts. *"And in this place I will give peace."*   Haggai 2:9

For the earth will be filled
With the knowledge of the glory of the L<small>ORD</small>,
As the waters cover the sea.

Habakkuk 2:14

Because of this, God is looking for those who will make themselves available to carry His glory into all the nations.

As He showed me one day as I was praying, He has enough glory for all of us, so you and I can go forth, taking up the mantle of Jesus and becoming intercessors for others, even as He sits at the Father's right hand making intercession for us.

Of course, this doesn't happen automatically. It requires a certain level of willingness, a certain level of commitment, and a lot of perseverance to bring it about. It also takes a consistent dedication to prayer and to God's Word, and, what is most difficult for many, a laying down of much that has been important to us individually in the past, so that we can embrace His perfect will for our lives today.

It took me time to grow into this place of usefulness in the Kingdom, but in time, it happened, as I was *Growing in the Glory.*

Carol Hylton
Brooklyn, New York

At Divine Gospel Tabernacle, Brooklyn, NY,
where I am presently ministering

PART I

BEGINNINGS

CHAPTER 1

MY SPIRITUAL ROOTS

I WAS ONLY THIRTEEN years old when I had an encounter with Jesus. I had been invited to a crusade held in our village in Trinidad, West Indies, and there God touched me.

I was one of six children, the third child of my mother. There were four boys and two girls in the family, and I was the younger.

My sister Shirley had invited me many times to attend that healing crusade that was being held in our community, and that night I finally said yes to her. It was a wise decision. When the preacher made the altar call for salvation that night, I went forward and was miraculously saved and also received my healing from asthma. God is so good!

There was a mighty presence of God in those meetings that birthed revival, and the songs, led by the evangelist's wife, were powerful. I still remember one song in particular. It said:

Where the healing waters flow,
Where the joys celestial glow,
Oh, there's peace and rest and love,
Where the healing waters flow! [1]

And, oh, how those healing waters were flowing!

Yes, I was born into the Kingdom during revival, and through that God placed a mark on my life that would endure, and I began to walk with Jesus. Now, many years later, I look back and see a thread of tapestry being woven into my life. How wonderful!

After being baptized in water on Easter/ Resurrection Sunday, I felt as if I was married to Jesus. I had come dressed all in white and, along with two other young ladies, was entering into a new experience with the Lord.

Shortly after my water baptism, I was filled with the Holy Spirit, joined the church that had hosted the revival (Morvant Pentecostal), and began to learn all I could about God's Word. The church laid a good foundation for a teen-age girl.

CHAPTER 2

THE EARLY YEARS

AFTER I WAS FILLED with the Holy Spirit I had a great passion for the Lord. My friends in school saw something different in me. My teachers also knew something had happened to me.

It was not popular to be a Christian in that school, so persecution began, but I was so passionate for Jesus that I simply could not contain my newfound love for Him. Even my mother said that when I prayed in those days it was "too much."

I was learning about life as a young person, and like most young people, I had dreams. One of the things I enjoyed doing was singing, so I joined the church choir and started my musical journey. In time I was invited to sing, along with young people from many other churches, with Youth for Christ and, thus, began to be exposed to the greater Christian community. We sang in concerts and large productions, and that was a wonderful experience for me. I sensed that God had a great plan for my life, and if I could but trust Him, He would bring it to pass.

But just as God has a great plan for us, so the enemy, the evil one, the devil, tries to steal God's plan from us. I had to learn this truth early in my walk with God. There were times when I seemed to lose my way, but God's Word kept me — even in those difficult times. His Word spoke to me when I questioned my faith. There were days when I was concerned for my future, but God's Word was the answer that restored life to me again. Yes, in those early days of walking with the Lord as a new believer in Christ, I encountered many tests and trials of my faith, but God kept me through them all.

I discovered that our Christian faith was like hiking up a mountain. I sometimes went on hiking trips with my senior class in high school, and those trips were a real test of stamina. We had to use our leg muscles to climb the high mountains of Trinidad, and it would take us all day long to get up a mountain and back down again. Many of my classmates tired along the way and had to rest often.

Trinidad is located in the tropics, and the temperature can get very hot during the day there, in the high 90s. So we had to drink a lot of water to stay hydrated through the trip.

Some did better than others on these trips. In our class, there were some long-distance runners, mostly male, but one or two females as well. These individuals would run up the mountain and make it to the top long before any of the rest of us got there. I often remember this when I think about the trials of the Christian life. We all encounter mountains that we must climb, and we need strategies for how to climb them. We must get involved in spiritual warfare and know how to engage the enemy. We need to fight in prayer to defeat this enemy of our souls, for he is always trying to discourage us and take us out of the race God has prepared for us:

> *For we wrestle not against flesh and blood, but against principalities, against powers, against the rulers of the darkness of this world, against spiritual wickedness in high places.* Ephesians 6:12, KJV

Can we conquer our mountain? Yes, when we engage in prayer and spiritual warfare, we can not only survive; we can bring the devil's kingdom down.

My journey in life was just beginning, and I sensed that it would be a struggle, but that I could overcome and be victorious in the end.

CHAPTER 3

A MAJOR SHIFT IN LIFE

THERE WERE RELATIVELY FEW opportunities in Trinidad, and I kept hearing about those who had made the leap of faith, leaving home, family, and friends to make a new life for themselves in the United States. Many of them were doing well, and I somehow sensed that this was where my destiny would lie as well.

By the time I was in my early twenties, I had become convinced that this was God's will for me. It would not be easy, but I was sure that He would be with me and help me at every turn.

The time eventually came for me to leave and I travelled from Trinidad to the United

States with such a great desire to serve the Lord.

When I first arrived in New York, I found a job in sales. I also did baby-sitting and house-keeping, anything to pay the bills while I worked on getting my immigration papers together, find a good church to attend and otherwise get my bearings.

Some other friends I knew from Trinidad were in New York, as well, some from our old Youth for Christ ministry there, so, in time, five of us got together and stated a singing group that we called Grove of Living Light. We sang in churches, schools, social functions, weddings, concerts, and youth meetings. We were also on radio and television and made our first musical recording. It was the beginning of my exposure to the music world.

Chapter 4

Marriage

DURING THIS TIME I met a man named Earl Ralph Hylton, Jr., and my life was forever changed. I was in my mid-twenties by then, and we were two opposite who attracted each other. After just three months of dating, there was no looking back for me. My singleness was over. Earl called me his "Jewel," as in "Pearl of great price."

We had a beautiful traditional wedding with many guest. I carried a white Bible under beautiful orchids, and a soloist sang the Lord's Prayer. We sensed God's presence with us.

Among the guests at the wedding were the Kitzes, a Jewish family I worked for in Long Island. The grandfather, Jacob Feldman, was the person I was caring for at the time. He faithfully attended synagogue every Saturday, and my time with that family placed a special love in my heart for the Jewish people and for Israel.

But I was not to be with the Kitzes much longer. Just one month after the wedding, I started working for Symphony Bridal Veils in New York City, where I had bought my own bridal headpiece. My boss, Maury Weis, and his wife Doris ran a bridal headwear and accessory business in the garment district off Seventh Avenue. The Lord had spoken to me in a dream and said, "Go and ask him for a job." I was hired that same day as a biller typist. I was just beginning to know the voice of God.

Fortunately for me, Earl was a U.S. citizen, so my immigration worries were also soon over. Then, after about three years of marriage, our son William was born in the summer of 1980. By that time, my status had changed, and I had become a permanent resident of the United States. I now had a lot to learn about motherhood.

Getting married and having a son had not dampened my desire to serve God. That desire only increased in me more and more, and now I was awakened to the call of God upon my life. Unfortunately, this caused some division in our family. In the end, my darling husband walked away from us, and we were forced to go on without him.

Deep feelings of rejection and abandonment now forced me to turn to a life of prayer and fasting. I wanted to see Jesus in a new way in my life, and this motivated me to pursue Him in a greater way through attending Bible schools and learning more about Him.

William and I spent a lot of time in the church we had settled upon, Calvary Pentecostal in Brooklyn. He was dedicated to the Lord in that church, and attended Sunday school there. I took advantage of all of the classes the church offered. One of the ministries I served in there was called Rhema. Those of us who joined memorized whole chapters of the Bible and then declared them before the whole congregation. Our leader, Phyllis Marrain, was a real visionary. Many Christians grew in their faith because of that ministry. I was one of them, and I eventually became one of the ministry leaders.

There is a price you pay for carrying the Gospel, and we must count the cost before we take up the mantle and run with it. This was my personal experience learning to lay down my life daily and take up the cross. The Lord has promised:

For I know the thoughts that I think toward you, saith the Lord, thoughts of peace, and not of evil, to give you an expected end.
Jeremiah 29:11, KJV

I began taking classes in Christian Counseling at a local Bible school (Brooklyn Tabernacle Deliverance). I was now working at CitiBank in Customer Service during the day time, and attending the classes at night.

CHAPTER 5

INTRODUCED TO CPT

IN 1988 REV. WALLACE Heflin and Sister Jane Louder came to minister at our church, and later that year I had the opportunity to go to their campground in Virginia (Calvary Pentecostal Tabernacle, or CPT as everyone calls it). My life was never the same after that experience.

Brother Heflin and his family had a vision for the nations, and they had gathered there in Ashland, Virginia people of like vision and were busy training people and sending them out to work for God. Their services were heavenly and challenging, and I grew in God every time I was able to attend.

Some of us went to their winter campmeeting that year for three days, and I experience a breakthrough of joy and victory. A new impartation of God's glory came upon my life, and it's been increasing ever since that time.

At a later time, I was invited by my friend and prayer partner, Sister Hollister Zacharie, to go to the camp in Virginia for a longer period. This time we spent a whole month there. It was a glorious time of prayer and fasting and learning.

Brother Heflin had taken a team into Kenya in East Africa, and God now said that He was making me "a watchman on the wall" for that nation.

On Sunday mornings we went with the group to their church in Richmond, and there we sang on the radio with Sister Sally Brown. That first Sunday night Brother Heflin handed me the microphone, and I was able to give an exhortation.

I remember getting a prophetic word from Mother Heflin, the Founder of that ministry.

"Jesus says He loves you," she declared, "and He is depending on you."

It was pleasure to serve in the camp office and also in the camp kitchen. I remember praying there one day with Sister Marilyn Govender, for her husband David, who was still in South Africa. There was revival going on in that kitchen, and it was not just for natural food service, but for a visitation of the Lord. We could break out in song or dance anytime the Holy Spirit moved, and there were downloads from the Glory realm for which I am so very grateful. I'm still living out today the things that God spoke to me in those days.

After we had returned to New York, there was a new strength that had come into my life, and I felt that whatever God asked me to do, I could do it. As our dear leader, Reverend Wallace Heflin, would say, "Just do it!"

CHAPTER 6

THE CALL

IN 1990, WHILE I was studying in Hugee Theological Institute, I was writing my first exam when God spoke to me. It was at the beginning of the Gulf War in Iraq, and He said He was sending me back to college to get my education in the health field.

In my mind I thought, "Well, I could study nursing because such skills are always needed in wartime," but God had other plans. Instead, I started studying Recreation in the Nations. My pursuit of nursing was eventually lived out when I graduated from Community Health, but something else happened to me during those years that forever changed the course of my life.

Incidentally, during my college years I served as the President for our Christian Club on Campus, but it was something else that is most important to this story.

Before I get to that, around this time I shared my camp experience with other sisters, and we took a trip down there together. One of the speakers for those special meetings was Rev. Harold McDougal, who has become my editor and publisher for this book.

CHAPTER 7

JOINING END-TIME HANDMAIDENS

IT WAS DURING THIS time that the call to become a member of the End-Time Handmaidens and Servants came to me. Through reading a book entitled *Daily Preparations for Perfection*,[2] I became fascinated with the life and ministry of Founder Sister Gwen Shaw. Born in Canada, she had dedicated herself to Christian ministry very young and went to Bible school. Soon after graduation, she was off to serve God in China.

Those were difficult years, and with the coming of the Communists, she was eventually forced to move to Hong Kong, where she worked for many fruitful years, principally among the Chinese refugees.

Then, something very dramatic happened to her. She was led to enter into a lengthy fast, and during that fast her heart was set on fire for the nations. She was just one woman, when women were not well received in ministry, but she obeyed God and blessed many nations in the process.

I completed my requirements for ETHS membership by doing the required twenty-one fast before I was ever able to meet Sister Gwen personally. When we finally did meet, at Blue Mountain Christian Retreat in Pennsylvania, I told her about an encounter I'd had with an angel during a time of prayer, and she said to me, "That's our end-time angel."

I had been experiencing quite a lot of exhaustion in my body from doing spiritual warfare, and suddenly one Sunday morning I felt the touch of that angel, and my strength was supernaturally renewed. That angel had travelled with me ever since.

One thing I have always remembered about Sister Gwen, who passed away before this book could be completed, was that she brought you into the presence of God. I loved being in her presence, because I loved being in His presence. When I told her I was writing a book, she gave me a lot of encouragement.

In addition to the twenty-one day fast on nothing but water, we were required to read two of Sister Gwen's books. One of them was her life story, *Unconditional Surrender,*[3] and the other was called *Love, the Law of the Angels.*[4] It was a wonderful beginning of my preparation for going to the nations.

It was the spring of 1991 when I completed my fasting, and the glory of God began to fall. That summer we traveled to Canada, Virginia, New York, and then St. Louis, Missouri, for the End-Time Handmaidens and Servants World Convention. It was there that I, along with other inductees, said my vows (the prayer of dedication) to become an End-Time Handmaiden. Part of that prayer said:

Lord, send the fire and burn up the sacrifice, and give me a double portion of Your Spirit.

He heard that prayer.

I was also ordained for the ministry by International Minister Forum. "It's not for man to say what I should or should not do for you," were the words the Lord spoke to me that day.

There was a stripping that came after this experience, almost like going into the wilderness. I suddenly felt a barrenness that I could not explain. I came to the conclusion that this was a preparation for things to come. Our Lord takes us through a wilderness experience so that when we begin to minister, it is not of us, but of Him. This was a time of rejection, misunderstandings, trials, and the testing of my faith.

CHAPTER 8

FORMING GOOD AND LASTING FRIENDSHIPS

BUT GOOD THINGS WERE also happening. I had been led to volunteer as a counselor at the Christian Broadcasting Network' 700 Club Prayer Center in New York, and while working there under the director, Apostle Roger McPhil, I met two other ladies with whom I struck up an instant, but lasting, companionship. They were Fay Montgomery and Maria Colon. Before long, we would be working together in Brooklyn, but we would also work together all over the world. The first ministry we started together was called

Daughters of Zion, and God was using us in prayer, intercession and worship.

In that atmosphere of prayer at the counseling center, God sealed our relationship, and we began a ministry that would take us around the globe. When I had started following my heavenly Bridegroom, I had no idea that I would be blessed to travel to many countries for ministry, and I had no idea how much the anointing of God on my life would cost me. Soon enough I was to begin a missionary life.

It was also in that prayer center, I believe, that I received a burden for Israel.

One day God gave me a word for the center. He said, "I told Joshua, 'As I was with Moses, so I will be with you.' " Immediately following this, the ministry changed hands and crossed over to became a local prayer center run by the director and his team. It was now renamed CHN, Christian Hope Network, and the three of us continued ministering there on the phones as counselors.

CHAPTER 9

HARVEST CHRISTIAN CENTER

BY 1994 I GRADUATED in Community Health and did some field work at Lenox Hill Health Education Center in New York, then I began working as a consultant in the recreation field. I worked in senior centers, doing recreation programs such as folk singing, storytelling, and folk dancing.

This was right at the season when Sister Fay was led to open Harvest Christian Bookstore and then Harvest Christian Church, and the Lord sent me there to help her. God had great things in store for us, and much land to conquer. This was the fall of 1994 and the spring of 1995.

During the early months after the Harvest center was opened, we had many visitors and guest speakers. I remember Sister Jane Lowder and David and Marilyn Govendor from Calvary Campground coming there. We also had Siggi Oblander and Sister Thelma Oney from Kentucky (they were connected with End Time Handmaidens). We were a new ministry, and God was sending us some of His choice ministers to help us lay the foundation.

I remember when Pastor Tom from The Vineyard Ministry came to minister to us. What a presence of God he brought! This was right at the height of the Toronto Revival with John and Carol Arnott, and we had the opportunity to go to Toronto to experience the renewal first hand and bring it back to Brooklyn. Many who came to those meetings were refreshed in the presence of God.

The river of God began to flow, and revival was in the air. There was a great thrust and hunger for more of God, and we began to experience revival in our souls. Those early days of the ministry came with great excitement, and many fellow Handmaidens came to partake of the glory of God that was being outpoured, receiving in the process an impartation that jump-started their own ministries. It was a time of the birthing for new things in God.

At that time, New Hope, led by Pastor Roger, was about four years old, a church birthed out of the activities of the 700 Club. On the day the prophetic word came that there would be a church coming forth from the counselors, I was one of those who were called out to help with that ministry. For the next four years, I was one of their intercessors and carried the burden of the work in prayer.

When the Harvest Center had opened, the word of the Lord to us was: "Do not despise the day of small beginnings," and God brought us to our next step.

At one of the meetings in the Harvest center I was slain in the Spirit and God began to give me a vision of a bridge. He said that I should build a bridge and make it safe for His people to walk over. I was also to make embankments. I saw that all the time the bridge was being built people were walking across it. Some fell into the water, but they reached out for help from others who were swimming. I could not speak all during this encounter, but I understood it to mean that Christians were to make it safe for Jewish people to come to the Lord.

One day I had an open vision in the bookstore in which Jesus appeared to me in a bright light. He came as the "Door," and He said, "I am opening a door for you that no man can shut. Walk through this door, for I have provision in it for you. It's an effectual door." A bright light covered me the whole time He was speaking this to me.

I remember saying, "Please, Lord Jesus, don't leave." This was the beginning of many such encounters with the Lord Jesus.

Once you have a face-to-face encounter with the Lord, you are never the same. And He has never left me; He's been there all the time, Thank You, Jesus!

In this way, God was showing up in His glory giving me directions for my next step. I had begun traveling to the nations a few years before, and now that would greatly increase for God's glory.

In Lower Manhattan, New York, NY

PART II

TO THE NATIONS

CHAPTER 10

MY FIRST TRIP TO JAMAICA

MY VERY FIRST MISSIONARY trip from the United States was to Jamaica in 1989. That year they were celebrating forty years of the University of the West Indies, and two of us sisters travelled to Kingston with Bishop George Bloomer and his amour bearer. We stayed just one week.

My girlfriend Violet gave her testimony to the women in prison about the miraculous birth of her daughter. It was a moving experience that left a mark on their lives. Her daughter, Rochelle, is now married and has a baby girl of her own.

Although it was such a short trip, it whetted my appetite for ministry among the nations. I knew that God had greater things in store for me.

CHAPTER 11

TO TRINIDAD

MUSIC HAD LONG BEEN a part of my experience and so while I was in Calvary Pentecostal Church I joined a group of ladies known as The Choral. We were backed up by an all-male band. The group was so well received that we made our first Album called "We Sing Praises."

That summer The Choral traveled to Trinidad and Guyana with Pastor Roberts and Sister Mavis, his wife, and a team of twenty-two. We experienced great revival and healing on that trip.

In Trinidad, my youngest brother, Joe Roberts, heard a word that changed the course of his life forever. He soon came to the

United States, where he met his wife Winifred, and they now have two daughters, Anna and Charis, my nieces. This was just an example of how God worked in my obedience to follow His call.

CHAPTER 12

TO GUYANA

ON OUR WAY TO Guyana, our plane encountered so much turbulence that it shivered like a leaf. The flight was forced to land in Caracas, Venezuela, and we spent the night there praying in the airport. The next day, they brought another plane to take us on to Guyana.

When we arrived in Guyana there was a great heaviness over the Land. This was soon after the tragedy of Jim Jones and his followers there. We sang songs and prophesied to redeem the land, and we did spiritual warfare over the atmosphere.

The call is great, and many are called, but few are chosen. We must have a listening ear to answer the call of God upon our lives so that we can fulfill His work in many places. I was ready for more.

CHAPTER 13

TO TRINIDAD AGAIN

IT HAS ALWAYS BEEN a blessing for me to go back home and visit my family. In the summer of 1996 Pastor Fay said to me one day, "God is calling you home to Trinidad." I prepared myself to go on special assignment. William was with his dad at the time, so I was free to accomplish my mission.

When I arrived at Piarco Airport in Port of Spain, my brothers Mc cord and David Roberts met me with the family. After greeting them all and getting reacquainted after so many years, I made an appointment to go visit Senor Pastor Allister Alexander, whom we called "Doc," and his wife Lula at the church where I had been baptized. Their new building had been recently finished, and they had taken on a new name — Daybreak Assembly.

The last pieces of furniture needed for the building were the pews, and God sovereignly sent someone to give the pastor US $10,000 for their purchase. It was a wonderful edifice for the glory of God.

The building was three stories tall and also housed a post office and a doctor's office. What a great vision God had given them! I felt blessed to be able to be a witness at the dedication service, and it was glorious. Rev. Turnel Nelson, the General Superintendent for the Pentecostal Assemblies of the West Indies, was the speaker. I also prayed on the third floor in the choir area and decreed blessings upon the music ministry.

God opened many doors for me in the three weeks I was there in Trinidad. I was invited to minister for Bishop Michael Lewis from Port of Spain, who had hosted our team on an earlier missions trip to some of his outreach churches.

God gave great favor with his people all over Trinidad. It was a wonderful beginning. Many came to the Lord in those services and God used me to encourage some of the younger pastors in the ministry.

Our footsteps are ordered by the Lord, and when we move in the timing of God, many lives are changed for His glory. It is wonderful to know that He can help us to be in His timing, because it is His timing that is perfect.

I was able to connect with many other family members during that trip, as well as the body of believers in Trinidad. What was ahead for me could only be the best. My dream was coming true.

CHAPTER **14**

MY FIRST TRIP TO ISRAEL

MY FIRST TRIP TO Israel was like a dream. I saw signs everywhere saying WELCOME HOME, and I felt like the beloved coming home to meet my bridegroom. I was stepping into the reality of a prophetic word that had been given over me seven years before.

It was the fall of 1996, and I had been on a forty-day fast when God spoke to me to go. On the fifth day of the fast, He said, "Come up to Israel. There is one spot left just for you." During the Ladies' Convention in Ashland, I had spoken with Irene Breadlo, one of the speakers that year. She was working with Sister Ruth Ward Heflin (from CPT in Ashland, Virginia) in Israel. She told me I was welcome to come and stay with them in their mission house in Jerusalem called Halcyon House.

God had arranged every aspect of this trip for me. Seven years before, a prophecy had come at a Full Gospel Businessmen's luncheon, saying, "You will walk in the footsteps of Jesus."

I was very excited, as you can imagine, that I was finally making my first trip to that wonderful land. And I was also excited that I would be going via London, England.

My ticket money had come in for the airfare from New York to London in a miraculous way. As we were coming back home to New York from our annual End-Time Handmaiden's World convention, held that year in Chicago, God did the work.

In the convention, prophesy had come through Cindy Jacobs saying that there would be "a changing of the guard," and that God had given us our new marching orders. The flight we were travelling back home on was overbooked, and they asked us if we would be willing to give up our seats. In exchange, we could travel home first class the next day, plus receive the cash sum of four hundred dollars. That was the first miracle I needed. In this way, my travels by faith began.

Now I only had to believe God for the balance of the fare from London to Tel Aviv, and God came through with that too. I was invited to preach the Word of God in our home church (Harvest Christian Center) and received a love offering that covered the rest of the trip. In hindsight, God was teaching me to trust Him every step of the way. I have done that, and He has never failed me yet.

As the Scriptures ask: *"Who is this coming out of the wilderness leaning on her beloved?"* It is I. Praise God. I was Israel bound.

I was also very excited about my stopover in London, another first for me. I landed at

Gatwick Airport, and there met one of our End-Time Handmaidens missionaries.

It was a short visit. Later that same day I boarded a flight from London's Heathrow Airport bound for Tel Aviv. I had been fasting meats and breads, and the first piece of bread I had eaten in forty days would be taken in the Promised Land.

I was thrilled to arrive in Jerusalem, after taking a minibus taxi up from Tel Aviv. My drivers were two nice Jewish boys who took turns at the wheel during our journey. I immediately started to tell them of my love for Israel and how I often prayed for Jerusalem. The romance had begun the moment I set my feet on the Promise Land. It was a dream come true.

When I finally arrived at Halcyon House, which was close to the British Embassy in Jerusalem, I had barely put my bags down when the residents of the house gathered around me to pray. That first prayer released a great healing anointing and also a burden for fasting in the house. Several of those who lived there were healed, and another sister who was sick in hospital received her healing at the same time. This was the beginning of eighteen glorious days in the land of the Bible.

That first week, on the days when there were no scheduled worship services in the house, we traveled to see all the places where the Bible had recorded miracles performed by Jesus. The next week we travelled to the Sea of Galilee and spent a couple of days in that region. In that place, while we were on a boat on the Sea of Galilee, God showed up, and His presence filled me so that I could hardly stand on my feet. It was a visitation from the Lord. Jesus is still walking upon the earth today, and He is still showing up in the Galilee.

He showed up in the most unusual ways during that first visit to the land of Israel, and I have many memories. I remember walking in the Old City with our Jewish tour guide,

Moshe, originally from Chicago, and learning about the miraculous history of the 1967 War. In a kibbutz, I spoke with Sarah, a Jewish senior citizen, who was seventy-seven years old, and she told me about the many miracles of Israel becoming a nation in 1948.

How exciting it was to have many first-hand experiences about the birthing of this nation that God loves so intensely. He made a promise to the people of that land, that David would always have a son to sit on the throne, as long as there was such a thing as day and night (see Jeremiah 33:1-19), and He has kept that promise.

That year (1996) the Israelis were celebrating three thousand years of the City of David and God's covenant promises. Imagine being in the Holy Land at the time of that celebration! It was historic, and I was there to participate. It was a glorious experience, to say the least.

As we travelled through the land of Israel, I had many visitations from the Lord. On one occasion, we were on our way to the Galilee when we saw several rainbows. When these rainbows showed up, God reminded us of the promise He had made to His people so long ago.

All of our trips to the biblical sites were wonderful, but the services in the house on Mount Zion were absolutely heavenly. There we sang, prophesied, danced, and declared the word of the Lord over Jerusalem. It was an encounter like nothing you could ever imagine. I still remember dancing in my off-white lace blouse and skirt, prophesying over Mount Zion. It was a most glorious time indeed.

The spontaneous singing that went on there will always be a treasure in my heart, as I recall those days in Jerusalem and on Mount Zion. During that time, the word of the Lord came forth, saying, "From Jerusalem and Mount Zion to the nations I have given the word," and God began to fulfill that word in my own life.

I have been back to the City of Peace two more times, but that first trip established my first love and set the stage for ministry in many other countries.

CHAPTER 15

THE INTERLUDE

AFTER MY RETURN HOME from Israel, I was ordained as Associate Pastor for the Harvest Worship Center ministry. For a time, God allowed us to work with Apostle Carlos Lopez, who formed the PASSION Network (Paul and Silas Strategizing International on Nations). After we had all prayed about it for a year, the network was launched right from the Harvest Bookstore there in Brooklyn. A little later, we moved the ministry to another of the five boroughs of New York, Staten Island. It was 1998, and we received a warm welcome from the pastors on that island.

Staten Island is like no other place in the five boroughs. It is surrounded by water and a lot more quiet than the other four boroughs. It is one of the high points on the Eastern Seaboard that stretches from Maine to Florida. There is a lot of history there — from Colonial Richmond Town, Historic Richmond Town, to Snug Harbor and Mariners Harbor.

After we settled in and began to get to know the community, we got acquainted not only with our neighbors, but also with the area churches and began to meet with area pastors. Since we had moved over the bridge we met to pray once or twice a week, and Pastor Fay was hoping I would be a second driver. I'd had my driver's permit for the longest time, and I just needed to take the necessary tests.

We were attending a pastors' meeting once a week with Bishop Joe Matera in Brooklyn, and I asked the pastors present to lay hands on me and pray that I would pass that test. They did, and when I went to take the test, I passed, and got my long-awaited driver's license.

The churches on Staten Island were a special blessing to me, and then we started our own pastors' meeting once a week in our new facility on the island. We had several ministers who came to pray with us weekly, including David Beidel, Pastor of New Hope Community Church. Brother David wrote the book *Samaria, The Great Omission.* After that year, God blessed him with his own church building.

Our facility was also used to house Upper Room Ministries, a ministry lead by Pastors Vincent and Grace Salerno, formally also of Brooklyn.

The building we secured for our ministry there on Staten Island had been a double-occupancy doctor's office. When the renovations began for the sanctuary, and the concrete floor was laid, we placed scripture verses in the foundation. At the dedication of the building, we had two prophets present who sang and gave forth the word about a future connection with work in the land of Israel.

That fall we had more than two thousand women gather for prayer in Madison Square Garden. Women of all denominations were joining forces to pray. They were from New York, New Jersey, Connecticut, Pennsylvania, and other places around the nation.

God said:

Where there is no vision, the people perish.
Proverbs 29:18, KJV

While all of this was transpiring, I was preparing for my next trip to the Holy Land. God had spoken that we would go back and forth, and one day there would be a ministry house in the land raised up to benefit His Jewish people.

CHAPTER 16

BACK TO THE HOLY LAND

MY SECOND TRIP TO Israel, in 1999, came about because Dr. Shaw invited us all to the first End-Time Handmaidens International World Conference in Jerusalem. The featured speaker that year was Derek Prince. Three of us went from our church, and we were blessed to see the land again, and also blessed to go via France. I still remember the French cuisine we were fed on the plane. It was very delicious indeed.

God favored us again in that we were able to go back to Halcyon House on Mount Zion in Jerusalem for three days before going on to the Holiday Inn Hotel for the conference.

Another of the conference speakers was Dr. Bahjat Batarseh from Jordan. He brought us up to date on the medical condition of King Hussein of that country. We also got a chance to mingle with some of the press representatives, and they gave us the latest news about the then-prince Abdullah, who would assume the throne upon his father's death.

The music at the conference was magnificent, with Pam Singer and Bertha and Barry Segal. There were other speakers at the conference, such as Israel and Effracene, a ministry team from Israel.

After the conference had ended, we saw more of the land. Israel is always a special place to visit. We went to the Western Wall and then to Samuel's Mountain. There will be a showdown in the near future between the god of this world and our God of eternity, Jehovah, just as the prophet Elijah provoked an encounter between the false prophets of his day and Jehovah God on Mount Carmel (see 1 Kings 18:21).

We again travelled to the Galilee to visit our friend, Sister Irene. I was baptized in the Jordan River, just like Jesus, even though it was rather cold that day. It was a wonderful trip, and I am happy to say that God's name was glorified.

Finally, before leaving, we were able to visit the House of Peace, a new ministry of End-Time Handmaidens in Jerusalem, and to pray for the release of finances for them to buy the building they were renting. It was soon purchased by the ministry and, on my next trip to Israel, we were able to stay there.

That winter we had the pleasure of welcoming Sister Gwen and her staff, Sister Sharon and Brother Philip Buss, to our ministry in Staten Island. Many handmaidens and servants came to that meeting from the surrounding areas. We had a full house, and God gave us our new marching orders through Sister Gwen.

As we approached the end of the year, God was about to close out my travels with a climax by sending me back to my African roots.

CHAPTER 17

TO KENYA

IT WAS IN JANUARY of 1999 that I made that second trip to Israel and by November of that same year I was invited to Kenya in East Africa. The Lord said to me, "You must put your feet on African soil before the century ends." He knows how to keep us in step with His plans.

I had met an African Bishop at Calvary Campground in Virginia that summer. He was in the U.S. on official business for his country. President Daniel Moi of Kenya had sent him to meet with our President Bill Clinton. I was led to tell the bishop that I was coming to Kenya, and we prayed for his meeting with President

Clinton. We also prayed for his wife, who was still in Kenya.

We never know how God will provide for our trips. I just knew that I was going to Africa, and I needed money for my ticket. In the end, my oldest and youngest brothers and their wives gave matching funds for the ticket. It was a God thing.

So away I went to Kenya with a team of six, four men and two of us ladies. The team was led by Rev. James Lay of Tennessee. Wow! I, from Trinidad, West Indies, the land of the humming bird, was travelling to the Motherland, Africa. How awesome God is to show His power!

We made a stop in Holland on our way to Kenya. When we got to Nairobi, the capital of Kenya, there was a lot of smoke circulating in the air from the cars and trucks. It was a true Third-World country. We made our first stop in the capital when we visited a small church. As we entered the building, the women of the church took me by the hand and did a circle dance with me. It was quite unexpected, but what an awesome experience!

Shelly Baker, a fellow End-Time Handmaiden from Missouri, had given me a prophetic word two years before in which she said that Kenya and Uganda would open to me. God had kept His word again.

When the time came for me to minster, two couples from Uganda arrived at the meeting. They had been travelling for two days to get there. That day I laid hands on every person in that assembly. What an awesome presence of God showed up in Kenya!

God is a God of timing. He is an on-time God. He may not come when we want Him to, but he's always on time.

God provided a college class on site, connected with the University of Kenyatta where we were staying. They were studying with their professor during the day, and they held prayer meetings early in the morning.

They later joined us in the African crusade that was held in Kitale. The crusade lasted for about ten days, and many were blessed by the teaching and preaching ministry and later submitted to water baptism. After God's name was glorified in Kitale, we went back to Nairobi.

On our last night at the hotel in Nairobi, the bishop I had met in Virginia sent his driver to pick me up, and I was taken to the palace to meet President Moi. Unfortunately he happened to be out of the country at the time. That night I met the bishop's wife Joyce and their two sons at his home and church and some of his members.

The next day I was invited to preach at a noontime prayer service in Nairobi, and the bishop's wife served as my interpreter into Swahili. God is so good!

The people of Africa gave me many wonderful gifts, and it was a great experience to get in touch with my African roots.

There was a great glory revealed in Africa. I still remember how every night the worshipers would dance and sing before the crusade for about four hours, and the glory would fall.

At different times in our lives, we all have appointments to keep. My appointment in Africa was very pivotal, because it was at the turn of the century and just before the new millennium dawned.

CHAPTER 18

Y2K AND 9/11

AS WE CAME INTO the year 2000, the changing of the century, many were concerned about the possible effects of the Y2K phenomenon. As we all know, we escaped — for a little while at least. Threats still hung in the air.

In November of that year Concerts of Prayer for Greater New York (COPGNY) was hosting a conference in Queens, and Pauline, one of the staff members, invited me to lead a delegation up to the World Trade Center.

That summer Passion Network, led by Apostle Carlos Lopez, had hosted Prayer New York in Central Park. Prior to that, just before the turn of the century, Rodney Howard Brown had come to

Madison Square Garden with an evangelistic crusade for six weeks. God was visiting the Northeast with evangelism and also the prophetic.

Cindy Jacobs from Generals of Intercession gave a word at Bay Ridge Christian Center in Brooklyn: "Something is going to happen in the Financial District, and when it does the church needs to go." As I was leading my team up to the Twin Towers for prayer, the thought never occurred to me that it would be the last time my feet would stand atop those great buildings.

That day we rode the train into Manhattan from Queens to the Financial District, and we made two stops. The first was in midtown at the Empire State Building, and the second was at the World Trade Center.

When the delegation ascended the elevators from one building to the next and finally reached the top, I remember looking out over the Hudson River and standing to pray with the rest of the team. On that high place I made many proclamations and decrees, while my team members stood behind me and laid their hands on me. It was an awesome experience with the power and the fire of God falling with a tangible presence.

We up all went to each of the four corners at the top of the building, praying and prophesying over New York City. God loves New York, and He was giving us New Yorkers a chance to repent and turn from our wicked ways. No destruction comes without warning.

On that dreadful day of September 11, as the Twin Towers fell, I was reminded of the prayers that had gone up over nine months before, and I believe God spared many lives as a result of them. For the lives that were lost, we will always carry sadness in our hearts, and we pray for the families that mourn.

Let us obey God:

Wherefore, my beloved brethren, let every man be swift to hear, slow to speak, slow to wrath. James 1:19, KJV

God is in the saving business, He gave a promise to Joshua:

As for me and my house, we will serve the LORD.   Joshua 24:15, KJV

We can claim that promise for ourselves too.

Post 9/11 Benny Hinn and his team came to New York City and held a crusade in Madison Square Garden. In that meeting, the glory of God was falling so that when Brother Benny spoke he was amazed at how God's glory was filling the auditorium. There were at least two thousand people outside who couldn't get in, so he went outside to greet them.

A dear sister, Merri Turner, was at that meeting, and she invited me to go with her to the Waldorf Astoria Hotel. She was considering using their facility to promote the First Ladies Tea in New York. While we were looking at the ballrooms, she decided to use her guest pass so that we could stay one night. Then, God blessed us with a second night's accommodations there. After Benny Hinny prayed for us, we left fully charged to go on to our next assignment.

Sister Turner was in the process of hosting a 9/11 event in Baltimore, Maryland, and she needed help. God put together a team of two doctors, a pilot, a chaplain, and many other volunteers. It took roughly two months before the project was completed. It was a great project that allowed us to hand out invitations at the Congress, the Supreme Court, the Pentagon, and at the various international embassies in Washington, D.C. This all culminated with prayer at the memorial site, the Baltimore Orioles Stadium, on September 13, 2003.

We made some very good connections along the way, and God sent us resources as well to complete the task. We flew over the stadium on 9/11, had communion, and sounded the Shofar. During the two months leading up to this event, we met with the pastors and the mayor of Baltimore at their regular prayer breakfast.

We also attended many area house meetings. It was a time of remembrance and God gave us some of his special servants to mark the event.

We can never forget that day, September 11, 2001, when tragedy struck the United States of America and the Twin Towers were destroyed, the Pentagon damaged, and many lives stolen from their families and friends. The nation was invaded on that day, and when I think of it, I still shed a tear because of such great loss. The freedoms we enjoy in America were threatened and are still at stake.

We sent a prayer up for all the families that lost their loved ones. Whenever we remember and look back on those days, there is always a sobering feeling that comes with it. It was a time to reflect on what God had brought us through and how He would move us forward.

Chapter 19

To Korea

WE WERE MOVING AND growing in the glory of the Lord. Now God's glory showed up in Asia, as it had in Jerusalem and in East Africa. It was 2003, and I was boarding a flight for South Korea via Alaska. I was on my way to visit Dr. Paul Yonggi Cho's church in Seoul.

I had been invited to go on a mission trip to Burma, and as I was praying about that invitation, I heard a word from the Lord, which said, "Come." God blessed me with a special gift to make the trip possible, this time it was from my tax return. After Korea, I would head to Thailand, to meet up with my team, and together we would travel to Burma, modern-day Myanmar.

Our mission to Myanmar was a special one, and it was also very dangerous. We would be taking Bibles into that very needy mission field.

It was a Sunday in March just before the war in Iraq when I visited that famous church in Seoul. There I experienced a most beautiful worship being lifted up unto the Lord. The dance ministry performed that day with great excellence, giving glory to God. Because the services were translated into seven different languages at once, thanks to my earpiece I didn't miss a thing.

Korea was all that I had heard about and more. I was so blessed by the ministry there and blessed to see that its foundation was prayer. God was preparing me before I travelled to Thailand and Burma.

CHAPTER 20

TO THAILAND

BEING ABLE TO TRAVEL to Thailand was God's special grace for my life. I have always tried to study the countries I will visit, and I had learned, among other things, that Thailand was still ruled by a monarch. Aside from that, I knew that it was important to hear the voice of God in any mission field.

I felt safe as our flight approached Bangkok. God had sent special angels to accompany me, but I didn't understand their presence until I got there. Then I felt them by my side.

Our team members, Denise and Kevin Reid from Four Corners Ministry, met me on arrival at the airport. My roommate for the trip was

Deborah, a lawyer from Chicago. She loved to pray, and so did I, and so we took that as our special assignment. We prayed for the nation and for our team members.

Other members of the team had gone into Vietnam, and we received word that some of them had been refused entry, so we began interceding for them.

Our time was to be very limited in Bangkok. In just a couple of days we would be traveling on to Myanmar to give out Bibles and do apostolic, prophetic conferences, but we knew that we had an important work to do right there in that huge city as well. God's call is always on time and always for a great purpose.

While there in Thailand, I was heartbroken to see the prostitution of women and little children. Jesus had said:

The harvest truly is great, but the labourers are few: pray ye therefore the Lord

*of the harvest, that he would send forth
labourers into his harvest.*

Luke 10:2, KJV

That was true everywhere, but who knew
about the depravity of the situation in Bangkok?
It was a place of such great need, and so we went
immediately to the streets.

The many bars lining the streets of certain
districts were open, and adult men were luring
children into them to be abused for their pleasure. I had never seen so many young women
and children caught up in human trafficking.
We ministered to as many of them as we could.

These young women needed the love of
Christ so that they could come out of that life-
style. It was heartbreaking to see them being
exploited in this way. On the streets of that mean
city, God began to open my eyes to the needs
of humanity, and I understood more than ever
why Jesus had died. His Word declares:

*And the Spirit and the bride say, Come.
And let him that heareth say, Come. And
let him that is athirst come. And who-
soever will, let him take the water of life
freely.* Revelation 22:17, KJV

When I answered that call in my own life so
many years before, I had only a limited understanding of the needs of humanity for a Savior.
We are all lost and cannot save ourselves, and
that's why Jesus came, to save sinners. The
Scriptures teach:

*For all have sinned, and come short of the
glory of God.* Romans 3:23, KJV

How wonderful that were able to carry a
ministry of grace and reconciliation to these
people and to let them know that Jesus' love is
greater than all our sins!

CHAPTER 21

TO MYANMAR

ENTERING MYANMAR WITH BIBLES was a serious matter, but we made it through customs safely and were then able to bless the Burmese people with the Word of God and with our prayers. We know what the Bible teaches:

So shall my word be that goeth forth out of my mouth: it shall not return unto me void, but it shall accomplish that which I please, and it shall prosper in the thing whereto I sent it.   Isaiah 55:11, KJV

We had come believing in that promise, and we were not to be disappointed.

I soon had the rare pleasure of putting my feet into the waters of a hand-dug Burmese well. The story we were told was that the Buddhists would dig wells and find no water, but Christians would come after them, dig wells, and water would spring forth. That was no surprise to us. God knows how to provide water for His people.

Hudson Taylor, the great missionary, had travelled to Burma so many years before and left a great history of work for the Lord, having served the Burmese people more than fifty years. We saw one of the original buildings where he had done his missionary work.

We had the great opportunity to wash the feet of the women of Burma and to prophesy over them at a women's conference. This had been the ministry of Jesus, when He took a towel and the basin, and washed the feet of His disciples:

After that, He poured water into a basin and began to wash the disciples' feet, and to wipe them with the towel with which He was girded.   John 13:5

It was truly an honor to wash the feet of the modern-day saints in that land, and we were grateful to God for having allowed us that privilege. During our stay in Myanmar, we also saw many miracles of God's provision.

We learned about the twelve tribes in Myanmar and about the many Buddhists who now desire to know Jesus. Three hundred Buddhist monks were fasting in Yangon, when they somehow got hold of the *"Who is Jesus"* video and came to faith in Christ.

I will have to say that I have never seen believers any more passionate for their faith than those in Myanmar. This trip was preparing me for my future appointment with revivalists of an earlier time. My experiences were all preparing me for a future that would lead straight into the history books.

CHAPTER 22

TO ENGLAND — TWICE

MY FIRST TRIP TO London was for a women's conference hosted by Judy Johnson. That was when I met Helen and Ian Harvey, a true End-time handmaiden and servant, who hosted me and my roommate for a week in their home in that great city.

Thomas Manton, IV was the featured speaker at the conference, and so I met him. I knew his father, who was a congressman from Queens, and I knew his mother as well. When I was in college, I'd had the opportunity to do my field work for his father's political campaign. He won the congressional seat that year. It was a wonderful conference, and God gave me a word for the Esther anointing, which Prophet Thomas released over the Women.

Six months later, after much prayer, I was invited back to London, but this time I went there for prayer, spiritual mapping, and intercession. God had me on a journey, and He had planned my schedule, for He knew that I couldn't plan such a journey all that well by myself.

Helen had seen a vision of me walking on the north coast of England at Norwich and invited me to come and travel with her there. I decided to go to England for three weeks, but God extended my stay to two months. Before it was over, I had my own flat provided for me in Hampton Court in London, and from that place God began to launch my ministry. The only name I had on my business card at that time was Called and Chosen/Bridge Builder (from John 15:16).

When Helen told me about the vision, it was the very place where the fishermen would bring in boatloads of people for the revival in the early nineteen hundreds. When we got to Norwich, I went and put my feet on that area to pray on the beach. God had told Joshua:

> *Every place that the sole of your foot will tread upon I have given you, as I said to Moses.* Joshua 1:3

I started walking in a new level of faith as I advanced on my journey.

I love libraries, and so while we were in Norwich, Helen and I went to the library there to do some research on Bank Plain (my prayer assignment) the Barclays Bank, which was being converted into "The Youth Project." We learned some interesting facts about the Barclay family tree.

One John Gurney (1755-1809), a reformer, a banker, an abolitionist, and a Quaker was married to Catherine Bell, whose mother was Catherine Barclay. We found a prayer book on intercession written by John Gurney in the

Library. He was also used to go to the United States Congress in Pennsylvania to petition an end to slavery back in the 1800s.

I was invited to go and pray for the youth project. This turned out to be quite an interesting project. The trustees for the project believed that God would use a certain old building to meet the needs of some of the youths who gathered on the weekends from the universities in the area. The cost of the renovation project was about ten million pounds, and they had secured about 2.5 million, so we had to pray in the partners (MP) to fund the balance.

Since that time the building has been renovated and is up and running 24/7. Glory to God! The power of prayer and intercession really works. Many challenges faced us along the way, but God always came through in the end. As God's Word promises:

I can do all things through Christ which strengthenth me. Philippians 4:13, KJV

The project trustees graciously hosted me during the week I was praying in that region. It was wonderful to learn about the vision God had given them for a Bible school, among other projects, to oversee. It was truly a time of seeing God's vision on another level!

CHAPTER 23

TO WALES

AFTER THIS ASSIGNMENT IN Norwich, God took us to Wales in 2004. It was the One Hundred-Year Celebration of the Welsh Revival.

While in Wales, we had the opportunity to visit Reese Howells' Bible school and see first-hand the original building for that school. It was in the process of renovation. There was an elderly lady in her nineties who was still alive from his ministry. This was the rich history of revival that God allowed us touch, and He allowed us to place our feet on that same soil.

The book, *Reese Howells, Intercessor,* [5] had been a great inspiration to my life when I first read it in the Harvest Bookstore. A great fire had been lit in me for revival and prayer in those days. Never did I dream that I would walk upon the grounds and experience first-hand what God started through a man like Reese Howells, who was so sold out to God.

Our next stop was at a retreat for ministers in Wales, where we visited an eight-hundred-year-old church. Such history was too wonderful to behold, and that's where the song of the Lord came to me. I began to sing, and it flowed out of me like a river — the classical hymns of the Church. Revival was a reality in the nation of Wales.

We stayed at a home for minsters, and our hostess was a lady minister from the Church of England. Her husband was a retired banker whom God had apprehended for the ministry of music. God is still looking for men and women in whom He can place the fire of revival, as He did with Evan Roberts in the Welsh Revival. It had been exactly one hundred years before when God started the

Welsh Revival through Roberts, and I was walking on that soil to inherit the fire of God for revival.

It was at this point that I got a call from Helen, saying that she had booked my ticket, along with my companion, for Israel. God had sovereignly ordered my footsteps to travel back to the Holy Land once again.

CHAPTER 24

TO ISRAEL THE THIRD TIME

WE WERE FLYING INTO Tel Aviv at the end of May and beginning of June, just in time for the Feast of Pentecost, the anniversary of the day the fire fell at Pentecost. The Jewish people call it *Shavuot,* and it is a time of harvest.

Our flight went through Italy this time. As had become my custom, every nation I put my feet on, I claimed for the Lord. The great Roman Empire was not out of God's reach, so I began to decree and declare there, "Let God's Kingdom come, and let His will be done over Rome."

We had a special assignment on this trip to Israel. I had been praying for six months for a sister who wanted to dedicate her son in Jerusalem.

When we arrived in Jerusalem, God provided for us to stay at the End-Time Handmaidens' House of Peace. There were six of us on this trip, and God gave us favor at every step of the way. We had wonderful accommodations, good food, and a wonderful assignment from the Lord.

Arriving in the House of Peace we had the opportunity to participate with a week of worship and scripture reading. It was called Harp and Bowl and was led by Rick and Patty Ridings. It was wonderful to proclaim the word again in Jerusalem.

We soon met a couple who were going once a week to the Temple Mount to pray, and they were willing to take us along. There we would dedicate the son. We met them at the beginning of the week and were planning to go with them that Thursday.

I was reminded of when Abraham offered up Isaac on Mount Moriah, for it was on that same spot where we would pray. As always, the enemy tried to sabotage our time of prayer and dedication, but God prevailed, and we were able to accomplish our assignment that day. He is Jehovah Jireh, the God who provides (see Genesis 22:14).

After the dedication, we went to the Wall to pray, and two of our brothers took the boy to meet the local rabbis and get their blessings.

At the end of that week the couple who had assisted us told us they had been very refreshed by our presence and were renewed with strength to continue their mission in the Land. I had always felt a call to pray for Israel, but that trip renewed and increased this desire in me. It was 2004, and the harvest was coming in whereever we went.

CHAPTER 25

BACK TO LONDON

AFTER TRAVELLING BACK TO London, my companion and I had an opportunity to attend a prayer gathering in Westminster Chapel. It was the June 2nd celebration of the Queen's Jubilee. I saw the need for intercession, as many ministers gathered for prayer. There were divine connections at that meeting that have continued until today. And it was a great opportunity to pick up the burden for the Church in England.

Later on, I was ministering to a couple from the Methodist Church in Hampton Court. That dear couple were lay ministers who were Spirit-filled, and they had a great desire to see God's people experience the baptism of the Holy Spirit. The sad fact, however, was that the senior pastor of the church they were working with did not believe in the infilling of the Spirit, and the couple was persecuted for their beliefs.

So many times we see the different camps in the Church warring. Here it was Pentecost Sunday, and God's power was given to the Church to be a blessing, yet the enemy fought the saints so that he could bring division.

Let us not be ignorant of the devil's devices. If he can divide us, he will win the battle.

Paul wrote:

... lest Satan should take advantage of us; for we are not ignorant of his devices.
2 Corinthians 2:11

Sometimes it is just fear that keeps a person from being filled with the Holy Spirit. The book of Acts declares:

And when the day of Pentecost was fully come, they were all with one accord in one place. And suddenly there came a sound from heaven as of a rushing mighty wind, and it filled all the house where they were sitting. And there appeared unto them cloven tongues like as of fire, and it sat upon each of them. And they were all filled with the Holy Ghost, and began to speak with other tongues, as the Spirit gave them utterance. Acts 2:1-4, KJV

God is still pouring out His Spirit today, and those who believe can receive.

On Pentecost, on *Shavuot*, the ingathering of the harvest, God wanted to fill His people afresh so that we could be witnesses of His power and demonstrate His Kingdom. He taught us to pray:

Thy kingdom come, Thy will be done in earth, as it is in heaven. Matthew 6:10, KJV

That precious couple had relatives in Israel, and I had been able to bring greetings to them and also to minister to them on this trip.

Living in London was a great experience, and when it was time to return to America, it was very hard to leave because we had become so attached to the community of believers there. One of the African pastors whom we had the opportunity to minister to took his leadership team on a retreat and called them to prayer because he was so blessed by our time there in London.

God accomplishes His mission on many fronts, because, as Jesus said:

The harvest truly is great, but the labourers are few: pray ye therefore the Lord of the harvest, that he would send forth labourers into his harvest. Luke 10:2, KJV

I must admit that the work of the Lord has been challenging for me, but also very rewarding. Little did I know I would be back in London within a few short years.

I was heading back to the United States with a heart of thanksgiving for all that God had done in those two months. I would spend some time with my family and wait for my next assignment. God had new connections for me. It was to be a season of getting connected with my Haitian family.

CHAPTER 26

TO TRINIDAD AND TOBAGO

IN 2006 GOD TOOK me back to my home-
land, Trinidad and Tobago, on a whirlwind
missionary trip. He has a way of taking you back
to your beginnings or your Jerusalem. This came
about through my brother, Patrick Phillip, who
had married Nelly, a woman of Haitian nation-
ality, and their son Matthew, my nephew.

While still serving in Staten Island, the Lord
spoke to me and told me that I had unfinished
business in Brooklyn. When Fay said that God
was sending her to Pennsylvania, I was not led
to go along. Instead, I moved in with Nelly and
was soon introduced to her pastors, Rev. and
Mrs. Paul of El Shaddai Haitian Church of God

in Brooklyn. They invited me to minister and later to be part of their staff.

I invited a friend, Sister Lenore Mason, to come there and speak. Sister Mason and I knew each other from Calvary Campground, but even before that, when she still lived in New York.

When she came to the church, she invited anyone who would like to join an upcoming missions trip to Trinidad, and the Lord said to me, "How about you?" And so I went.

There were four of us, and we had VIP treatment for the first two days. What I didn't know was that God was about to reconnect me with some of my senior classmates from the high school I was attending as a girl when I first had my fiery encounter with the Lord.

There were only four of us from the U.S., but a home team was prepared to help us, and some of them turned out to be my former classmates. They were now saved and very much involved in ministry, and they were happy to see how God was using me all over the nations. Who could have imagined it all?

I prophesied over some of them before I recognized who they were. That was truly an awesome and amazing encounter. The fire fell, and God's glory showed up like rain. The revival had begun among my peers.

In the days to come, we traveled all over Trinidad and Tobago, preaching, teaching, and prophesying the Word of God, with signs, wonders, and miracles following. Some of the most important cities we visited were Port of Spain, Toco, San Juan, and Arima Sangre Grande. At some of the churches where we ministered, they had steel orchestras with drums, the music of the Islands, and it was very enjoyable.

I could sense that God was preparing me for things to come in England, Jamaica, and Haiti. These were yet on the horizon.

After spending our last days in Tobago, we returned to Trinidad, and I was able to have a special time to visit my family just before returning to the

United States. This would be the last time I saw my oldest brother, Vernon Modest. He had served as a Councilman in his earlier years in Belmont area near Port of Spain, the Capital of Trinidad. It was a very strategic trip, especially for Vernon. We prayed together and then bid him farewell, and he soon went to be with the Lord.

CHAPTER 27

TO HAITI

IN THE BEGINNING OF 2008, while I was serving as the English Pastor for El Shaddai Church, God spoke to me that I would be going to Haiti. It had taken me a year to finally agree to start their English Service, and it was not long before I began praying about going to their country, all the while, bringing in ministries to encourage the congregation. Many fivefold ministers came to the church during that season, but I kept praying about visiting Haiti.

The climate in Haiti at that time was not conducive for missionaries. It was not until February of 2008 that God finally released me to take a mission trip to Haiti. It was my first, but it would not be my last.

My first experience on the soil of Haiti reminded me so much of Israel that I called the country my Petite Israel (Little Promised Land). I felt the same love for this land that I had for Israel on my first trip there. God had said:

Ask of me, and I shall give thee the heathen [nations] for thine inheritance, and the uttermost parts of the earth for thy possession. Psalm 2:8, KJV

When I arrived in Haiti and met my host family, I felt a kindred spirit with them. I began ministering in the mission church in Haiti, El Shaddai in Bertie Petionville. For twenty-eight days we prayed, prophesied, taught, and preached the Word of God there.

This was my mission field, and I had entered it with very little knowledge of Creole or French, the language spoken in Haiti. But God had sent me to Haiti with the pastor's wife, and she served as my interpreter.

On that trip we ministered at a wedding ceremony and reception, where God showed up in a wonderful way — all to His glory. He knows how to "dress the bride" because we are His Bride, and He is coming back for us one day.

I also had the great opportunity to do a women's conference called "Women of the Bible." I gave out the characters of the Bible with some of the corresponding scriptures to the ladies in the congregation, and they had the opportunity to act out their various parts.

Wow! Those ladies came out in rare form, bringing those characters to life. They were characters like Eve, Sarah, Deborah, Rachel, Esther, Ruth, Naomi, Elizabeth, Mary, Phoebe, and others. It was a wonderful conference, and God was showing me all the talent in those ladies that was locked up, just waiting for someone to come and release them.

Everywhere I went, I felt that same love for the land of Haiti, and I felt like Abraham when he was going to inherit the Promised Land. God had said to him:

Get thee out of thy country, and from thy kindred, and from thy father's house, unto a land that I will shew thee: and I will make of thee a great nation, and I will bless thee, and make thy name great; and thou shalt be a blessing.

Genesis 12:1-2, KJV

God has an inheritance for each of us, if we will just be willing to go after it. We must say, "Yes, Lord, here am I. Oh, Lord, send me!"

The last Sunday before I left Haiti, I ministered that day in El Shaddai Mission Church. We lead the congregation in a prayer for blessings upon Israel and upon the land of Haiti (see Psalm 122:6).

CHAPTER 28

TO ENGLAND AGAIN

BY THE END OF 2008 I was travelling back to London and on the first day of 2009, I found myself arriving there again. My friends, Helen and Ian, would be my hosts for the first four weeks. God is faithful in all that He does and is doing in our lives. It was a blessing to be with this missionary family that serves God in the nations of the world.

They had a new addition to their family, a son, Gideon, who was eight months old and just a lovely baby boy. A miracle of prayer had brought him forth, and what a blessing he was!

As the days passed, we visited Norwich, where Helen's parents were living, to see some of our prayers that God had answered.

Back in London, I had been praying about an invitation I received from Bishop Shoshanna in Slough to visit her church, and now we went. On our first visit to the church, we were blessed and invited back the next Sunday to minister. God had sent me to England in the midst of a financial crisis to bring a word of faith. He has said:

A word spoken in due season, how good is it!   Proverbs 15:23, KJV

A word fitly spoken is like apples of gold in pictures of silver.   Proverbs 25:11, KJV

After I released that word from God in the assembly, great encouragement came to God's people. Many of the brethren felt the peace of God descended like a blanket. Jehovah-Nissi came to cover His people.

I was blessed to be used that trip in many areas, even praying an End-Time Handmaiden program called Redeeming the Land. The significance of the program is achieved by taking communion while praying over the land, as revealed in Sister Gwen Shaw's writing.[6] It was a real blessing.

God is a Restorer and a Provider for His people. He will move just like He did in the wilderness, when Moses was taking the children of Israel through to the Promised Land. The Lord said to Moses:

> *"I will make all My goodness pass before you, and I will proclaim the name of the Lord before you. I will be gracious to whom I will be gracious, and I will have compassion on whom I will have compassion."* Exodus 33:19

There is nothing too hard for our God. He is well able to solve our problems and meet our every need.

Many businesses recovered after my visit, and it was only because of God's faithfulness. Testimonies came from the family that hosted me of how God had restored their business and increased it even more. In fact, the testimonies are still coming forth about the goodness of God! He is a good God, and He wants to show us His goodness — if we will allow Him to.

My last great experience before I left the UK that time was to visit Windsor Castle. It was a great time because the State Rooms were open for international world leaders. Our tour guide gave us all the details of the rebuilding of some the rooms that had been necessary after the damage from the fire of 1992. The majesty and beauty of those rooms tells the story of that royal palace.

On a former visit, I had gone to Hampton Court, King Henry VIII's residence. My overall experience was tremendous. To have had a view of these palaces was a treasure I will always cherish indeed!

CHAPTER 29

To Jamaica Again

IT WAS THE SUMMER of 2009, and I was on my way back to Jamaica, West Indies. God was sending us back from America to be His witnesses there. He was giving me another opportunity to visit that precious land, only this time we went to Montego Bay.

We had a team of five ladies, from New York, New Jersey, Pennsylvania, and California. The team was led by Evangelist Zipporah Daley, and God had a special assignment for us in Jamaica. That assignment was to pray over the nation for rain, and for blessings. We also held a couple weeks of crusade in Bounty Hall, Trelawney, and Rose Hall.

God's fire began to burn on the altar of our hearts when we arrived in Montego Bay. That fire burned every night as we gathered for prayer to command the heavens for rain. We experienced deliverance and breakthrough on every front.

The angel of the Lord showed up, and God spoke a message through me, saying, "It shall surely come to pass! It shall surely come to pass!"

We held a crusade in the open air sometimes, and at other times we met in a tent. Oh, how God showed up in those meetings, where many were changed by His power!

During some of those open-air meetings, when I got up to minster, the glory of God fell while I was singing in such a way that the musicians could not stop playing. Eventually, when the message came forth, I remember asking the question, "Will you be a little donkey for Jesus, so He can ride on your back? God is looking for those who will carry the message of the Gospel. It is a humbling place, but if you are willing, God can use us to be His ambassadors."

That day I remember a whole ball club of young men giving their lives to the Lord. We say, "Yes, Lord, we are willing to be Your little donkey, to carry the Son of God!"

So many blessings of increase came to the churches where we ministered! Truly God is a good God. The report from Evangelist Daley was that one of those churches had doubled in size and another had tripled in size.

Before going home, we got a chance to take in some of the sights of Montego Bay. The sea water and the rivers there are so beautiful. God was good to give us some time to rest and enjoy the beach before leaving.

On returning home I spent a season, about three months, in prayer and fasting. During that time I was invited to speak at Abiding Love Ministries in Fredericksburg, Virginia. I ministered for their Eighth Year Anniversary Service in November of that year. Then I travelled back and forth for a while helping Pastor Margaret (Wilson) Bailey with her ministry.

CHAPTER 30

MY SECOND TRIP TO HAITI

IN DECEMBER OF 2009 I was still in Fredericksburg, praying at a noontime service with a small group at Abiding Love Ministry, when God dropped a burden of travail on my heart for Haiti.

It was snowing outside that day, and the roads were covered so that no one came in or went out. Suddenly I began to weep uncontrollably and shake while praying for Haiti. I didn't understand it, but that day I wrote in my notebook, "There is going to be an earthquake."

So violent were the shakings that day during my prayer time that my Spirit knew about the earthquake, even though my mind did not yet comprehend it. This happened because we are made in the image of God — body soul and spirit, and when our spirit is in tune with God, He can give us visions and dreams of things to come.

Bishop Gregory from Nigeria brought a message that day: "Do not weep, for the Lion of the Tribe of Judah has prevailed to open the seven seals." It was right on time.

After that meeting, my flight was booked from New York to Port-au-Prince, and in January, just two weeks later, I boarded a Delta flight for Haiti, just five days before one of biggest earthquakes ever to hit that island nation.

When I arrived in Haiti, I was reminded of a vision I had seen two years before, preparing me for my return. In that vision I saw little plants budding (like Aaron's rod), a picture of life coming forth from seeds that had been planted two years before, and of souls like shoots coming up in little pots.

I also saw that I was buying souvenirs. I knew then that I would return to Haiti, and now I was there.

I had invited Sister Zipporah Daley to accompany me, and she travelled from Atlanta, Georgia. When we arrived at El Shaddai Mission Church that next Sunday morning I introduced her to the congregation. After greeting the brethren, she invited the congregation to cry unto the Lord. God's Word says:

> *The LORD is far from the wicked: but he heareth the prayer of the righteous.*
> Proverbs 15:29, KJV

Therefore we ought to cry the more unto the Lord. This was just two days before the earthquake hit.

God's Word also teaches us:

> *But without faith it is impossible to please him: for he that cometh to God must*

believe that he is, and that he is a rewarder
of them that diligently seek him.
Hebrews 11:6, KJV

Diligence is a virtue, and we need diligence to advance in our faith.

This eleventh chapter of Hebrews, which we often call the faith chapter, begins:

Now faith is the substance of things hoped
for, the evidence of things not seen.
Hebrews 11:1, KJV

When we examine this chapter, we see many of the patriarchs of old overcoming through their faith. We, too, are called to walk by faith and not by sight, and are reminded that the Kingdom of God does not come by observation (see Luke 17:20). Growing in our faith, therefore, should be of vital concern to every believer, every born-again child of God — in Haiti and every other country.

As the days went by, we were invited to minister at a Church in Quix de Bouquet. On the day in question, after we arrived, we spent some time praying with the pastor and his members. The Scriptures say:

Who knows if you have come to the king-dom for such a time as this. Esther 4:14

Can a land be born in one day?
Isaiah 66:8, NASB

God has promised:

And it shall come to pass, if thou shalt hearken diligently unto the voice of the LORD thy God, to observe and to do all his commandments which I command thee this day, that the LORD thy God will set thee on high above all nations of the earth. Deuteronomy 28:1, KJV

But this is one of those promises where diligence is required.

This word *diligent* means "performing with intense concentration, focus, and responsible regard; industrious. A constant effort to accomplish something; attentive and persistent in doing anything; a diligent student." *Diligence* refers to "someone who is very determined and strong willed."

The person who is diligent perseveres, is attentive and responsible to make sure the task is done. Then, when the task is finished, they have a sense of accomplishment.

Before I returned to Haiti I had been using *Command the Morning in Prayer* [7] by Dr. Cindy Trimm for about three months. The requirement of diligence it promotes was a great preparation for the mission. The foundation was laid in prayer, so we were equipped for the journey.

This teaching was also important for us on the day we went to Quix de Bouquet. We arrived at the Church about four o'clock with Pastor Octomollier, who served as our driver that day. When we got there, we got acquainted with the pastor of that work, Pastor Johnny, and some of his members. The electricity, we had been told, only worked part of the day in Haiti, so we had a short time to do what we had been sent to do and then leave before sunset, or there would be no lights to show us the way.

We began to pray very passionately, a prayer of repentance for the sins of Haiti, contending for righteousness, when what sounded like a loud shofar was heard. We had laid our hands on the pastor to pray when the building began to rise up and move forward. This happened once, then a second time, and then a third. By the third time, we were all outside.

What was happening? It was the big one, the 7.0 earthquake that had hit the Island, causing much devastation, and we were right in the middle of it.

When I saw the look on the face of Pastor Johnny, my first words to him were, "Do not be afraid," but the truth is that we were all amazed, astounded, and flabbergasted at what had just happened to us. Experiencing an earthquake is a traumatic experience, one that you can only recover from by the grace of God.

As we began to make our way back to the house in Tabbare, where we were staying with the Lerime family, we saw many people along the streets. Some of them were weeping, but others were praising God. The reaction was mostly fear, worry, and consternation.

The streets were crowded with people whose homes had been damaged or destroyed. There was a lot of chaos and confusion, questions, and a total interruption of everyday life.

We stayed for twenty-eight days after the initial shock. Little had we known that this was only the beginning of our mission.

When we finally got back to the house where we were staying that day, we found that every television had fallen over like the idols in the days of Gideon (see Judges 6:25-29). God was up to something good for the nation of Haiti.

That night almost no one slept in their beds. Most chose to sleep outside under tents for fear of new tremors. We slept inside in beds because we trusted God.

One nearby family had lost their baby in the quake, and others had suffered similarly. That night we started nightly meetings for the young people of the area. It was heartbreaking to hear their stories. Many had lost classmates in the tremor. Their school building was damaged, and, as a result, there could be no classes. These were the type of stories we were hearing.

We began going to the hospitals to pray for the sick and the injured. Many had lost limbs and through the force of the quake. Those who survived but lost their homes now sought shelter, and huge tent cities sprang up overnight to accommodate them.

We had the opportunity to pray for the supply of food and water to be restored in the affected areas. The shops and banks were all closed for about a week, and this added to the suffering. It was a great opportunity for the nation to repent and call on God.

Many families came to the place where we were staying and were fed, and God provided so wonderfully that they were able to take home bags of groceries with them when they left. It was truly brothers and sisters caring for each other.

We went to pray for a businessman who had a thousand employees. He and his wife and son lived in the mountains, and their house had survived. They were very open to our ministry of prayer, and God visited them in a special way.

Rich and poor ... we are all at the same level in times of disaster. Steve Green has written:

People need the Lord,
People need the Lord.
At the end of broken dreams

He's the open door.
When will we realize
that we must give our lives,
For people need the Lord. [8]

We went back to Quix de Bouquet a couple weeks after the earthquake. We intended to have a meeting that night, and to prepare for it we went out evangelizing during the day, going house-by-house to pray for the sick and share the Gospel. Some were healed, and some received Christ as Savior. Most were touched by God in some way. That night the little church was packed, and the message God gave me for these people was from Isaiah 60:

Arise, shine;
For your light has come!
And the glory of the LORD is risen upon
you.   Isaiah 60:1

After that meeting we went to buy a generator. The store, much like our Home Depot or Lowes, had been filled with generators before the earthquake, but now there were only six generators left. Thank God we were able to buy one of them for the church.

We ladies, two of us, were able to lift the generator and carry it to a taxi. Then we unloaded it when we got back to the place and presented it to the pastor.

We had a three-day call for prayer in the nation, and instead of the festivities of Carnival, there was a cry to God. He was visiting the land of Haiti with revival and the Church of God was being resurrected, after the shock of the earthquake. He had said:

If my people, which are called by my name, shall humble themselves, and pray, and seek my face, and turn from their wicked ways; then will I hear from heaven, and will forgive their sin, and will heal their land.

2 Chronicles 7:14

Anything that causes us to pray and seek God is good.

I had received a prophetic word from Chuck Pearce that said, "The wilderness shall bloom again, and the desert shall blossom!" God soon gave me new songs that I began to sing and teach others to sing:

God Said

God said He will fill His house with glory.
God said He will fill His house with praise.
God said He will fill His house with glory.
God said He will fill His house with praise.

God said He will fill His house with glory.
God said He will fill His house with praise.
God said He will fill His house with praise.
God said He will grant to us salvation.
God said He will grant to us His peace.
God said He will grant to us deliverance.
God said He will grant to us release.

As the waters cover the sea, so
the Lord will cover thee.
As the earth is filed with His glory,
so the Lord will cover thee.
God said He will fill His house with glory.
God said He will fill His house with praise.
He will raise up sons of glory, He
will bring the praise again.
He will raise up sons in Haiti, He
will bring the praise again.
God said He will fill His house with glory.
God said He will fill His house with praise.
God said He will fill His house with praise.
He will fill His house with praise.

RESTORATION

Restoration, restoration in
the glory of the Lord,
Restoration, restoration in
the glory of the Lord.

There is healing, there is healing
in the glory of the Lord.
There's deliverance, there is deliverance
in the glory of the Lord.
There is salvation in the glory of the Lord.
There's revival in the glory of the Lord.
There is peace, there is peace
in the glory of the Lord.
The peace of God that passes
understanding in the glory of the Lord.
Receive your blessings in the glory of the Lord.
The blessings of the Lord, it maketh rich.
In the glory of the Lord, it's all in the glory.
All that we need, it's in the glory of the Lord.
All that we need is in the glory of the Lord.

God was indeed at work in the land, and I was privileged to be part of what He was doing.

CHAPTER 31

THE HAITIAN RECOVERY

AS GOD WORKED, OUT of the ashes of this terrible disaster came beauty. His beauty began to show up right in the midst of the recovery.

During our twenty-eight-day stay after the earthquake, we saw many mighty miracles. Many got up from their hospital beds and went home healed.

Amazing miracles came from those who lived in the camps, how they would cook and help feed many of their neighbors. God was showing His faithfulness to us every day.

The earth continued to shake almost daily and, as you can imagine, this shaking caused a lot of fear. My sister–in–law's parents went through the earthquake where they lived in Port-au-Prince, her father was injured, and they began sleeping outside in a tent. All the houses to the right and left of their house had collapsed. The day I went to visit them, her father was finally getting medical help. Some paramedics from the flying hospitals came and took him to a hospital. (One of the first medical teams to arrive after the quake to help the Haitians was from Israel.)

El Shaddai Mission Church was not physically affected by the quake. The structure was made of sold rock, thank God. Jesus is the Rock, and He kept that building safe during the quake.

As you can imagine, our families and friends back home were very concerned for our safety during this time. Some reports even said that we had died in the quake. Some family members tried to make contact with us and could not. The fact that Haiti was still shaking gave them reason for concern.

One of my sisters-in-law, Winni, messaged me on Facebook and said, "Why don't you come home and rest? You can go back later, after you've gotten some rest." I think this message was what I heard in my spirit when I tried to leave prematurely.

It happened like this: There was only one night that I slept on the floor, and that night I heard the words, "Go home." Thinking that this was the Lord, the next day we went to the airport to board a flight, but there were no planes flying out of Port-au-Prince.

I met Franklin Graham and his team from the Samaritan's Purse at the airport that day. They had come to serve the people most affected by the quake. Seeing them made me realize that I had not yet finished my work and I must go back to my post to complete my assignment. There was no need to leave before the job was done. Diligence always endures to the end.

During the next couple of days we encouraged the pastors and their congregations in the

Lord. Many had to find ways to cope with their loss, and so we comforted the bereaved.

Worship helped to lift the heavy burdens from the heart of the people, so every night we had a time of worship and prayer under the open skies. It was during this time that the young people came forth with their best contributions. Those days were very important as the Haitian people began their journey of restoration and healing.

At the end of twenty-eight days, we had to travel back home from Santo Domingo, the Dominican Republic (the nation that shares the Island of Hispaniola with Haiti). Due to the fact that the airport in Port-au-Prince had been demolished in the earthquake, we still could not fly out from there. It took us a full day and night of travel to get through to Santa Domingo and get a flight out.

That flight was a great miracle because we had no tickets to leave from the Dominican Republic, but God showed up and made a way for us to board that plane back to New York (and at no additional charge). I am sure many who were leaving Haiti had similar circumstances, but I knew that our mission trip had been ordained by God.

We were going back to New York with a lot of emotion and gratefulness to God for His protection during that very difficult time. A young Haitian father who had lost his five-year-old son in the quake accompanied us back to New York. We had a lot to be thankful for. It had been a time we would always remember. God had protected us when we were not even aware of the danger. So many buildings had been destroyed, but we had not been injured in any way!

The Haitian Minister of Justice, whom we had met on a different occasion before the earthquake, lost forty-seven out of forty-eight employees. We later went to see that devastated area. We also saw the Palace in Port-au-Prince broken and fallen. It was a very sobering time, one that I will never forget.

One man testified that God kept him alive in the rubble for twenty-eight days. "Someone in white," he said, had brought him water every day.

Some people say there is no God, but the people who say such things have never experienced Him in difficult circumstances. God showed up in the most extreme cases for us, and He taught me so much on that trip.

His Word shows us:

The earth is the Lord's, and the fulness thereof; the world, and they that dwell therein.   Psalm 24:1, KJV

The Lord is thy keeper: the Lord is thy shade upon thy right hand.
                                        Psalm 121:5, KJV

And the Lord will create upon every dwelling place of mount Zion, and upon

her assemblies, a cloud and smoke by day,
and the shining of a flaming fire by night:
for upon all the glory shall be a defence.
Isaiah 4:5, KJV

The name of the Lord is a strong tower:
the righteous runneth into it, and is safe.
Proverbs 18:10, KJV

The Ancient of Days has a covenant with Haiti. Jesus showed up in a vision seen by one of His ministers. He was with the children in Haiti, and He said, "I care for them."

The music for the national anthem of Israel is *Ha Tikvah,* and it is included in the French Creole song books of Haiti. That is nothing but the root of David. The Diaspora carries ancestral roots for Israel. Once the connection was made to Israel, God's blessing toward His people was released.

We prayed the prayer to bless Israel and to bless Haiti (see Psalm 122:6). Those who bless

Israel will be blessed, and so we will continue to pray blessings over Israel. But we must also continue to pray God's prosperity over Haiti. Most churches pray the Our Father, *"thy kingdom come; thy will be done,"* but this prayer in the Psalms is another step in obtaining the blessings of God.

Let's not stop there, but let this prayer go forth from the nations of the world, so that the God of the covenant can bless every nation. On that great day, at the Marriage Supper of the Lamb, every kindred, every tribe, and every tongue will be there to celebrate with the Lord. Don't miss it!

CHAPTER 32

RETURNING ONCE MORE TO HAITI

IT HAD BEEN ABOUT nine months since the earthquake had struck Haiti, and the children had been out of school all that time because most of the schools were destroyed by the quake. It was time for me to return to that land, and what could I expect to find?

On a personal level, during the days after I got back to New York, my body had experienced a lot of trauma. I got overheated and experienced exhaustion, fatigue, and tiredness. It seemed like the grace for the mission had lifted, and physical signs and effects of the earthquake were manifesting.

During that time, one of my End-Time Handmaiden sisters in the Lord, Jovita Torres, invited me to come to her home in Jersey City to rest, and soon I began to get some release from the signs of exhaustion. Later I travelled to Ashland, Virginia, to Calvary Campground, and while I was there, God restored my body. So I was going back to see the brothers who were still recovering from the effects of the earthquake.

I spent several weeks ministering in El Shaddai Mission Church and in other assemblies in the community. Around that time the Lord had me writing a movie on "The First Miracle Performed in the Life of Jesus." This happened when Jesus turned water into wine at a wedding in Cana (see John 2:1-11).

Jesus and His disciples were invited to a wedding, along with His mother. When He got to the wedding, He was told that they had run out of wine. Mary, His mother, said to Him, *"They have no wine"* (verse 3).

Jesus said to her, *"Woman, what does your concern have to do with Me? My hour is not yet come"* (verse 4). We have a similar response sometimes when God is telling us that it is our time. Don't miss your timing!

It was then that Jesus stepped into the supernatural. He asked for six water pots to be filled with water, and then He blessed the water. The servants who witnessed the miracle knew the jars were filled with nothing but water.

Jesus then instructed them to take some of the water to the governor of the wedding feast. When the governor tasted the water, it had been turned into wine. He said, *"Every man serves the good wine first, and when the people have drunk freely, then he serves the poorer wine; but you have kept the good wine until now"* (verse 10, NASB). God is ready to serve His best now! You and I may be His best-kept secret!

The young people were meeting faithfully every week for Bible studies. God had seen their desire to learn of Him even during their times of distress, so when we introduced the movie script, they immediately responded with approval. We had rehearsals, costumes, music, camera, lights, action, and food. It was a wonderful celebration, just before they went back to school. Thus I have seen the thread of God's faithfulness, even in times of great distress. He is our Burden Bearer.

I was impressed with the talent those young people showed. Surely they will be great world leaders one day. Greatness lies deep inside each of us, but it is only when we tap into God's resources that we can know what is there. The Scriptures declare:

But all these [gifts] worketh that one and the selfsame Spirit, dividing to every man severally as he will.

1 Corinthians 12:11, KJV

We must go deep to find the treasure within us.

Not long ago I attended a wedding in New Jersey, and what was so amazing about the couple being wed was their willingness to put the necessary work into their marriage, to build a foundation upon God's Word. Marriage is a covenant, and we, as the Bride of Christ, are a picture, or example, of marriage. Jesus is our Bridegroom. Let us prepare ourselves as the Bride, so that when He comes we'll be ready, ready for His return. He has said that He is coming soon, to receive His Bride. Are you ready?

On the day of the earthquake, many lost their lives in an instant, so those young people in Haiti know the value of life. Life is precious, and we need to live ours by making the most of our time here on earth every single day.

Behold the bride groom cometh.
                            Matthew 25:6, KJV

This was the cry the five wise virgins and five foolish virgins all heard. The wise virgins were prepared with oil in their lamps, so they went in to join the bridegroom. The foolish, however, did not have enough oil, so they had to go out searching fore a place to buy oil for their lamps. When they came back, the door was shut, and they could not get it (see verse 10).

Don't be left outside. Start preparing now, so that you can be ready when the Bridegroom comes.

CHAPTER 33

THE POWER OF PRAYER AT WORK IN HAITI

IT IS VERY IMPORTANT to understand the role that prayer played in the rebuilding process of Haiti.

I was in Fredericksburg, Virginia, teaching at a noontime prayer service, and when I was finished giving the message, my ticket was booked for Haiti. Fredericksburg was the place where God had me start doing the program we called Redeeming the Land. There I had the opportunity to intercede on behalf of the blood shed on the land during the Civil War and during the time of slavery. During those days, the story of Harriet

Tubman became very real to me. The Lord was allowing me to enter into a time in American History that I had only read about.

While doing this, the call came to go back to Haiti in early 2011. I continued to travel in Virginia for a season, teaching and preaching, and then I went back to New York to get ready to leave for Haiti.

On this trip, God sent me for twenty-one days, to pray concerning the election of the new president. The first time the presidential elections were held, the outcome was inconclusive, so the process had to be repeated.

After the quake, there was urgency for new leadership, and the presidential race had a lot of contenders. Now it was narrowed down to a couple of favorites. God was picking His man, the one He chose to lead the nation. As it happened, he was a former musician, not a politician from the Old Guard. He was new to politics. After much prayer and some fasting, the election went on as planned.

The whole world was about to see God's choice, a young man who was a favorite of the people. When he had first been nominated, he was not yet a favorite, but we know that prayer changes things.

Once the election was held, we had to wait several days before the announcement of the winner was made. God told me, "The world will see My hand upon the land of Haiti," and so it was. Instead of chaos, the people were dancing in the streets when their new president, Michael Martelli, was revealed. Once again God was smiling on Haiti. After all of their sadness and pain, there was joy again.

The children were back in school taking their classes and getting their education. And the country was recovering because businesses had reopened, and commerce was moving forward again.

Recovery was on the way. Even the people in the tent cities were moving out to more permanent housing. Most of the rubble from the earthquake had been removed. The power of prayer was at work as the people turned their hearts to God. Since then we have sent barrels of biblical resources into Haiti to meet this spiritual hunger.

We held a women's conference on prayer and releasing the prophetic. God had showed us that He truly is a God who answers prayer. Many people have longed to see a change come to Haiti, and God gave us the opportunity to see it. It was the beginning of better days to come for that nation.

Later we were invited to meet with Mr. Martelli at York College in Jamaica, Queens, where I did my senior studies in Community Health. I had VIP tickets to go and meet the new Haitian President personally and give him and his wife a book on prayer.

The president publicly recognized the importance prayer played in his campaign, and when he hosted the unveiling of his vision for Haiti there in New York, he reserved a whole wing for pastors. He shared the vision with Haitian Americans with such hope that we could only pray that God would bless his administration and bring the vision to pass.

With God, all things are possible. When we invite Him into any situation, in any nation, His Word promises:

Blessed is the nation whose God is the Lord. Psalm 33:12, KJV

We look forward to many future travels to Haiti and to the other nations of the world.

And he said unto me, Thou must prophesy again before many peoples, and nations, and tongues, and kings.
Revelation 10:11, KJV

As for Haiti, we pray that God will continue to reveal His plans and establish that nation on right principals. Let us all pray for those in authority, that it will also go well with us and there will be peace in the land (see 1 Timothy 2:1-2).

At Nicole and Delano's wedding in New Jersey.

PART III

TODAY AND TOMORROW

CHAPTER 34

THESE GLORIOUS DAYS WE LIVE IN

I AM VERY HAPPY to be living in these days in which God is revealing His Glory in new and wonderful ways and taking those of us who are willing from glory to glory to glory. His glory is being revealed in His Church, His Bride. He will have a Church washed in His blood, holy, and spotless. He will have a Bride that He has ordained for Himself and whom He will glorify for His name's sake.

We are being prepared in these days to go with the Bridegroom, so there is a transformation taking place, as we go from glory to glory.

One of the marks of the end-time Church is that we will look more like our beloved Jesus. We are the Body of Christ manifested on the earth. We will have His qualities and attributes. The fruits of the Spirit will be evident in our lives. The gifts of the Spirit will be in operation in us.

Are you a part of the Bride? Jesus is our Bridegroom, the Lamb of God, the Lamb who was slain. In the days to come, we will be known for our passion and our dedication to the Lamb:

These are they which follow the Lamb whithersoever he goeth. These were redeemed from among men, being the firstfruits unto God and to the Lamb.

Revelation 14:4, KJV

There will be a company that follows Him wherever He goes. Those who are set apart for the purposes of God will be used in this day, and they will do great exploits.

Jacob, who became Israel, was one of the patriarchs. When he encountered the angel of God one night, he said to the angel:

I will not let you go unless you bless me!
Genesis 32:26

Jacob had this glorious encounter during a time of severe trial. He had been running from his brother, Esau, for some twenty years, was about to meet him again, and wasn't sure what the outcome might be. It was that very night that Jacob wrestled with the angel and God blessed him.

It had taken Jacob twenty years of searching to get direction from the Lord concerning his destiny. Now he was a new man, and so his name was also changed. He was no longer Jacob, but Israel.

Is there an enemy you are facing today? It could be sickness or lack, but armed with the anointing of God's Spirit you can face any enemy. You must no longer allow people or things to stop you from completing successfully your life's journey.

Who can contain the presence of the Almighty God, the One who created the entire Universe? He came with such power that there was instant combustion, and, although His plan was met with opposition on every side, nothing could stop Him then, and nothing can stop Him (and us with Him) today. God has a great plan for each of us, beloved. Just believe.

CHAPTER 35

WHAT OUR FUTURE HOLDS

MORE THAN TWO THOUSAND years ago now, Jesus came to this earth to save us, and we are still enjoying the free salvation He paid for with the sacrifice of His life. That sacrifice was not in vain. He made a way for us by laying down His life and taking it up again, when He rose again from the grave. Salvation is a free gift, but the price Jesus paid for us to have it was great indeed.

We are blessed today to be able to have a relationship with the Son of God and to be an heir, a joint heir to inherit the blessings of God's Kingdom with Him. He has given us a new life, yes, life everlasting.

If you have not done so already, now would be a good time to receive the life of God through His Son Jesus. Just invite Him in right now. Pray this prayer:

Jesus, I invite You into my life.
Come into my heart and be my Lord today.

Amen!

If you prayed that prayer out of your heart, He heard you and has answered. You are now His child. Rejoice, and start *Growing in the Glory*!

Resources

The Holy Bible, King James Version, New King James Version, and New American Standard Version.

Wikipedia.com, an article on the Welsh revival

Bridge Builder, a prophetic word from 2000

News reports of the Earthquake in Haiti, January 2010

End-Time Handmaidens and Servants Newsletters

ENDNOTES

1. Shaw, Gwen, *Daily Preparations for Perfection,* (Jasper, Arkansas, Engeltal Press: 1986).
2. Words by H.H. Heimer, music by Leander L. Pickett. First published in Louisville, Kentucky, by Pickett Publishing Company: 1902.
3. Shaw, Gwen, *Unconditional Surrender* (Jasper, Arkansas, Engeltal Press: 1986).
4. Shaw, Gwen, *Love, the Law of the Angels* (Jasper, Arkansas, Engeltal Press: 1979).
5. Grubb, Norman Percy, *Reese Howells, Intercessor* (Fort Washington, Pennsylvania, CLC Publications: 1997)
6. Shaw, Gwen, *Redeeming the Land* (Jasper, Arkansas, Engeltal Press: 1987)
7. Trimm, Cindy, *Commanding Your Morning,* (St. Marys, Florida, Charisma House: 2007)
8. Words and music by Steve Green.

EDUCATION

Carol Hylton studied in York College in Queens, New York, and at Kingsborough Community College in Brooklyn, New York. She received an AS degree in Community Health and was awarded a Gold Medal for Outstanding Community Service.

ON RADIO

Hear Pastor Carol on Good News Chronicle Internet Radio 26 at Court Street, Brooklyn. New York. (Figeroux & Associates), Attorneys at Law.

www.ingramcontent.com/pod-product-compliance
Lightning Source LLC
Chambersburg PA
CBHW031548040426
42452CB00006B/236